FROM THE HIP

A Concise History of Hip Hop
(in sonnets)

FROM THE HIP

A Concise History of Hip Hop
(in sonnets)

Stephen Cramer

Published by

WIND RIDGE BOOKS of vermont

Shelburne, Vermont 05482

Published by Wind Ridge Books of Vermont
PO Box 636
Shelburne, Vermont 05482
www.windridgebooksofvt.com

Also by Stephen Cramer:

Shiva's Drum
Tongue & Groove

For Mike B, my listening buddy all these years.

Contents:

2000s:

A QUICK NOTE, JUST BECAUSE

I've heard some people say that their brains hurt when they read sonnets and others that their ears bleed when listening to rap. My goal with this project was neither to hurt brains nor to make ears trickle with blood. I just love hip hop. I grew up on Beastie Boys and Run DMC, made it through the years of Vanilla Ice & Kris Kross, and continue to be astonished by artists like The Roots and Eminem. I also love reading and writing sonnets. I love the way that writing them makes you say things you didn't expect to say, and the way that every time you sit down to a sonnet, you get to see where the form wants to take you instead of leading the poem's content around on a leash. In the past few years I've found that I love working on them together. Let's face it, I'm also just drawn to the idea of mixing an eight hundred year old form with the unique content of the 20th and 21st centuries' pop culture. Each age is given its own unique set of images to work with. Basho was absolutely brilliant, but he couldn't possibly have written a haiku about an i-phone, or Public Enemy for that matter.

But Stephen, you say, *these don't look like the sonnets I ignored in my high school English class.* True, while each poem has the traditional fourteen lines (and seven sets of rhymes), in many ways I've departed from traditional sonnet conventions. For one, while many of the poems do stick to more traditional rhyme schemes such as three quatrains and a couplet, many of the rhyme schemes vary quite a lot. For another, instead of the slavish ten-syllable count for each line, I've allowed myself a little extra space here and there And of course I wanted to be sure that the poems were infused with the rhythms of natural speech, so I leaned heavily toward the language of the street instead of that of the classroom.

I should also add that this book is not intended to be a greatest hits of hip hop. Nor, needless to say, is it a complete history. This isn't even a list of my favorite hip hop tracks. It's simply the fifty-six songs from which the sonnets most naturally flowed for me. I would have loved to have sonnets about A Tribe Called Quest and Wu-Tang Clan. In fact, I wrote a half a dozen about Tribe, but in the end none of them really came together. It's too late for this publication, but darn it, maybe one day I'll nail that poem.

In the end, my hope is that someone intimidated by sonnets can pick up this book and relax because of the familiarity of hip hop's images, and that another person who might be intimidated by hip hop can take comfort in the formal gestures of the sonnet. I hope it's not just a weird conjunction, like lemon squeezed into a glass of milk, but more like the union of a disc of vinyl and a spiral groove.

—S.C.

1980s & BEFORE

The Apache Loop (DJ Kool Herc, 1975)

While twilight settles in the trees, Herc sets

    up two turntables & shoves the amp's

plug directly into the city's current

    as it bolts through the base of a lamp-

post. The crowd gathers, & he unsheathes his vinyl—

    two copies of Bongo Rock—& starts cutting back

& forth so quickly between the two tables

    & their continuous circuit of breaks

that the b-boys gasp for breath & his fingers

    blur. He drains so much juice that the lamp's gleam

stutters, strobing the night as it flickers

    & dims to the beat. But not even Herc dreamed

that whole cities in the days to come

would black out to this endless loop of drums.

Rapper's Delight (Sugarhill Gang, 1979)

Hank is moonlighting in a pizza joint,

    rapping to himself when he's taken outside

to an idling car. He doesn't disappoint

    in the back seat audition, so he gets a ride

to the big time recording studio

    to rap these verses he didn't write.

From there, the equation's simple. It goes

    like this: take Chic's most popular hit,

subtract the lyrics, keep the funky bass & strings,

    & overdub some new rhymes.

                These are

the good times, the women of Chic sing,

    but in a few weeks, those times are over:

disco is dead, the seventies are gone,

hip hop's ready to rise, *& time marches on.*

Can I Get a Soul Clap
(Grand Wizard Theodore, 1980)

It takes practice to see rhythm's fury

      ensnared by the tightly wound spiral

of the record's grooves. So, story

      goes, Theo's dropping the needle

on break after break when his mother

      busts in. The song screeches to a halt with the slur

of squealing wheels... Pause of disbelief, & he stares

      at that sound, the auditory blur

of the first scratch. So he works the record back

      & forth against the needle, building a new music

out of its own disintegration. *It's like*

      bombing a record shop, he thinks,

like tearing apart every sound I've ever heard.

Now it's time to resculpt the shards.

Flash to the Beat (Grandmaster Flash, 1982)

Flash scavenged junkyards for turntables, old

    needles & mic switches. He gleaned speakers

from abandoned cars, relished the smashed gold

    of radios that had been kicked to the gutter.

Then he carted them home for his mechanical

    autopsies: with a screwdriver

& a soldering iron, he'd dismantle

    them to see their tidy bowels—wire,

air coil, & battery—then hack

    them together, recombining

the de-funked pieces to bring them back

    to life, a mechanical Frankenstein.

Neighbors laughed, but he'd change music with what he'd made

from all the disassembled parts: the first crossfade.

Looking for the Perfect Beat
(Afrika Bambaataa, 1983)

The video cuts back & forth between

    what looks like a Mardi Gras from outer

    space & a dancer's jagged repertoire. It's *out there*,

even for New York. So imagine

Bambaataa's tour: he's in Paris, scratching

    off his records' labels so no one can

copy his cuts, though such a thing

    probably never occurred to the crowd; they stand

around like a herd of zebra airdropped

    into Times Square. Bam chants *we are the future…*

    After the concert someone asks, *You're*

from Africa? Then someone else: *what's hip hop?*

Bambaataa slowly shakes his head & smirks.

Next question. *Are there trees in the Bronx?*

It's Like That (Run DMC, 1983)
A Fan Makes a Skeptic Reconsider the
Cartography of Hip Hop:

You hear the track from that group I've been tellin'

you about?

        (Laughs) Nah, man, *real* hip hop's made in

the *Bronx*. I mean, come on... where the hell

is this place called Hollis? Nebraska?

I'm telling you, man: give it a listen.

Come on. These brothers went to *college*, yo.

This is about *roots*. I gotta ask ya:

what's hip hop without a ghetto?

Listen up. (He presses *play* & nods, transfixed

by a bass drum's double thump.) Not bad, right?

They've got some solid rhythms

Their lyrics

can be *too* smart.

But they still smack of the street…

(Smiles.) Alright, I admit: this group's better than most.

Next thing you know, they'll have rap on the West coast!

The Human Beatbox (The Fat Boys, 1984)
Two Fans Speak:

Are you sure that's just his mouth? It sounds like

    the cross between a scratched record & a mule in heat.

      Tellin you. The man, along with guys like Doug E.

        Fresh, is a bona fide pioneer.

        Of what? Eating his weight? He looks more

like the human *beef*-box. I don't mean to be cold,

but the guy's heading for a heart attack.

(Slaps him over the head with a rolled

      up newspaper.) Shut up, man. Ain't nothing funny

        about heart attacks. & yeah, that's his mouth.

      (Backing away) Ow, man, that really

        hurt. Still, you gotta admit. The truth

is: those guys are *big*.

          I've seen guys larger than that,

but I've never seen a group so phat.

It's Tricky (Run DMC, 1986)

Three card Monty with Penn & Teller

    goes like this: they take everyone's money, bracelets,

& jewels. Then Run DMC's chopper

    lands, & they strut the rain-slick street with their laceless

Adidas. They step up to the table, throw

    money down, & keep on finding the queens

as though the card were the size of their borough.

    They hustle the white men right back & bleed

them dry. Then, taking pity, they give them black

    hats & sneakers, & teach them their dance's spin

& gyration.

        The cloning complete, the chopper takes back

    off. Weeks later, radios in every suburban

kitchen are playing their song on the FM

dial, & all the little white boys look just like them.

Fight for Your Right (Beastie Boys, 1986)

The party's tame
        until the boys pile

    in, hammer the TV
           to shards, & spike

the punch. The three pull off
        the image of imbeciles

    so well that one can't
        be blamed for thinking

they're idiots.
        It must have been a joke,

    their first image,
        but separating the rapper

from the man is hard: like
        distinguishing smoke

    from fog, or trying to tell
        the couch dancer

from his dance.
        In the end, the room is fuming

    like the crashed Boeing
        on the album cover.
The stereo's still pumping,
        the bass still booming

as the three crawl out
            the door. But years after

they shed those personas,
            that night's ruins

will trail them, the party's smoke
            clinging to their skin.

I Need Love (L.L. Cool J, 1987)

In his white sweat suit—unzipped to reveal

    furrowed abs—& his Kangol hat, L.L. croons

the first rap ballad, in which he claims to feel

    ready to settle down, to stay in & spoon

with his lady (the background: no thumping

    bass, but a synthesizer's chimes). Cut

to: Georgia where LL's dry humping

    a couch while he mouths lyrics soft as velvet

& licks those baby lips. A swiveling crotch

    in private is fine. But he's nailed (public lewdness)

because he's up on stage, & the couch

    is a prop. L.L. scans the audience

for a girl to sing to...

                That night, the crew cleans

up, ready for the next town, the next crop of teens.

.

Push It (Salt-N-Pepa, 1987)
Two Misogynists Speak:

I know that they're one of the first

    female rap groups, but come on, yo.

Do they really have to talk about giving *birth*?

    Man, you're sexist. Have you seen the video?

        We're talkin' Spandex, knee-high red boots,

        & Spinderella throbbing in the booth

behind. Ain't nothing about labor in that song.

You sure? It's called "Push It." Man, it's just *wrong*.

    You need to listen to the lyrics,

        bro: *the music's pumpin' like I wish you would.*

        (Smirks) Tell you what: I'd pump Pepa if I could.

(Laughs to himself) *Now* who's bein' sexist?

    Whatever, man. This single's sick.

I can't wait to see what their next is.

Rhyme Pays (Ice T, 1987)
A Consumer Speaks:

What the heck's this sticker doing on my cassette?

    Parental Advisory? Okay, I'll buy

it after I ask my mom. Yeah right… I don't get

    it. What do parents need to be advised

about? It's *gangsta* rap, so yeah, it's explicit.

    I'm *paying* for the tape's f-bombs & slurs,

so the execs can sit there & dis it

    all they like. I mean, do they think this'll *deter*

people from buying the music? Hell no.

    & who the heck is this Tipper Gore

in the news? Her warning makes me want to go

    back & find some more censored tapes, or

heck, even buy out the whole section

just so I can start a rap sticker collection.

.

Parents Just Don't Understand
(DJ Jazzy Jeff and the Fresh Prince, 1988)
A Lesser Known Rapper Speaks:

He's the DJ & I'm the Rapper? Come on,

    man, this record's obviously aimed toward folks

who need to be told which of the black pawns

    on stage is which. I mean, just take a look

at the video: it's all sanitized

    & cartoon-like, the streets scrubbed down to

a sheen. This is the world on Lysol.

           & the guy's

    not rapping about swiping a few

bucks or his dad's last smokes. He's talking about

    stealing his parents' *Porsche* for Chrissakes. Look: his rhymes

are good, & the guy's funny, no doubt

    about that, but shoot… It's not like I'm

jealous of his mass, suburban appeal.

I just wish *my* parents had a Porsche to steal.

.

It Takes Two (Rob Base & DJ E-Z Rock, 1988)

This is the cut that the DJ spins

    at every wedding party, the girls

    in their satin & grandmother's pearls,

the boys a blur of cufflinks & grins.

        The dance floor floods at the first sound of that shuffled

rhythm. *So let's start…* everyone chants,

      it shouldn't be too hard…

              Fast forward five dull

    years: one half of the couple is straying

    & the other half has a one way

      ticket to the closest bar… But the lyrics' true

beauty is that singles can sing along, too: *I stand*

      alone, don't need anyone… It takes two

to make a thing go right, or so says the song,

but it just takes one to make it go wrong.

.

Fight the Power (Public Enemy, 1989)

The lyrics showcase Chuck D's politics,

    but the video mostly displays Flav's

lunatic persona: his crazy-eyed antics

    as he flashes a gold-toothed grin—*Yeah boyee!*—& raves

while the clock looped around his neck flows

    with his sway & counter-sway. The song's about

revolt, about how most of their heroes

    don't appear on no stamps. But however they shout

& politic, all people across the nation

    want to know is *what's up with the clock?*

    Chuck D don't care. (Go ahead, let them obsess.) Chuck

D knows that the train's pulling into the station,

because this is the end of the line.

He knows the clock & song both say: it's about *time*.

Pump Up the Jam (Technotronic, 1989)

Though she wrote & sang the song, Ya Kid K
was fifteen at the time & couldn't play
    the band's live shows. Enter Congolese model
    Felly Kellingi to lip-synch the vocals.

The kind director tailors the video
    by cutting from one shot to the next so
that she never has to fake more than two
    foreign syllables in a row.

Every shot's superimposed on a neon pink
    & green background, pulsating against the gauze
of faux sound waves. This is art as shroud: the graphics
    & their vertigo are meant to distract because

the woman the group supposedly sang with
doesn't even speak the language.

Fuck Tha Police (N.W.A., 1989)

A courtroom scene: the case is presided over

    by Judge Dre while Cube, Eazy-E, & Ren

make the case that uniformed men target their

    group because they're young & black. Even

when they're just standing on a corner,

    they say, they fit a profile: puffy jacket, shades,

a little bit of gold & a pager,

    so the men in blue take every chance to raid

their ranks & pat (or throw) them down.

                             The police,

    protesting the lyrics, refused to provide

their concerts security. But on its release,

    white boys by the thousands rushed out to buy

the self-proclaimed crazy niggers' album,

to have Eazy's gun pointed right at them.

Potholes in My Lawn (De La Soul, 1989) Trugoy the Dove Does an Interview:

That's right, sir, we're from Amityville, Long

    Island, an hour east of the City.

Yeah, *that* Amityville. But let's move this along;

    you don't need to make up some gritty

narrative about the fact that we

    come from the most infamous haunted town. Things

are scary enough out there.

                Like what? Really?

    How about the gun-toting rappers bloating

the scene? How about the spate of misogynist

    lyrics or all the drug-worship?

                  Sure, I mean,

you can say we have "spirit," though to be honest

    I think we're all sick of the pun.

We've got *real* issues beyond being "demon-spawn."

Let's start with the potholes in our lawn.

High Plains Drifter (Beastie Boys, 1989)

Ash-covered bricks,
        dangling shards—

    on the ramble through
        the Lower East Side, I clicked

photo after photo
        of the gutted & charred

    boutique. Later, I scroll
        through them like

the CD on repeat
        in my stereo.

    In the song, the cop
        pulls the band over

for speeding,
        demanding to know

    where the fire is. It's in
        you, in your lover,

in the road, in the burning
        roof & tower.

From my speakers,
        even the *lyrics* smolder,

    because all the boys can do
        to counter the furnace

of the world is belt out
                    this song. Flames may burn us,

door jambs may buckle
                    & floorboards boards warp,

but the beat is indifferent.
                    They let it drop.

1990s

U Can't Touch This (MC Hammer, 1990)

On stage, Hammer's pants are amebic: sleek

    or billowing, depending on the breeze.

The jaunty backbeat of *Superfreak*

    gives form to his liquid moves like a tide. He's

thrilled by the way he can start & stop

    the crowd's adulation with a roll

of his hips...

        On a tour of his mansion, he pops

    into a room with a remote control

waterfall purling inside. *Listen to this.*

    He closes his eyes as the water glances

off itself. *Sounds like a crowd clapping.* (Emphasis

    on the word *crowd*.) Another flick: silence.

The mansion's empty. Another flick & grin,

then the sound of applause starts up again.

Ice Ice Baby (Vanilla Ice, 1990)

On Arsenio, Vanilla's frosted

    pompadour is a miniature skate park

of bleach, his hair about as fluid

    as the frozen sea of sequins sparkling

on his suit. It makes sense: Robert Van Winkle

    was born on Halloween, so he loves costumes.

(Even the *yup yups* & *yeah boyees* he sprinkles

    his speech with are a kind of mask.) The room

is quiet. The crowd just wants to *woof woof*

    & pump their fists. But Ice needs to give proof

that he's legit. *Yup yup*, he answers

    with a grin. If others doubt, at least he's the best

in his own head. *& people said I'd never*

    amount to S-H-I- You know the rest.

The Humpty Dance
(Digital Underground, 1990)

Humpty's wreathed not in gold necklaces

    or leather, but in a polka dot tie, a white

        fur hat with its price tag still stuck

        on its back, & a plaid coat that looks

like it was tailored out of a prep school

    banner. He proclaims his physical allure despite

    all that, as he instructs the crowd on how to bust

    his new, off kilter dance: You just

limp to the side like your leg was broken…

                    Drool

        on, ladies. Let Humpty put you in a hex. He

won't bore you like some dumb Adonis. No, this

lover'll make you wiggle your asses

        with his new definition of sexy:

a plastic nose & Groucho glasses.

Everybody Dance Now
(C+C Music Factory, 1990)

In the video, Freedom's abs are as hard

    as his delivery (this is what Ice-T

would sound like if he decided

    to give up rapping about the street

in favor of the dance floor's bump & grind).

    The screen's bombarded with Zelma Davis' full

lips, gulfs of cleavage, caramel thighs. She'd signed

    on to lip synch Marsha Wash's vocals

because execs deemed Wash unmarketable

    (fat's not sexy, they said, even draped in *bling*).

In the wake of Milli Vanilli's scandal,

    Wash sued to be credited. The ruling,

simple: women can weigh what they please & get paid

like queens. *Is that dope enough? Indeed.*

So What'cha Want (Beastie Boys, 1992)

The filter warps
             Ad-Rock's whine to distortion,

exaggerates MCA's rasp
             which almost drowns

    the whorl of the organ's
                loop. The thermal

    video fizzles the cobalt
                sky to pixels

so that the landscape,
             through the ankle-height

    camera, approximates
                their contorted voices:

the spires of pines,
             like reverse lighting,

    shoot up from the ground
                as three city boys

ramble through the woods,
             spreading their arms (What

    cha *want?*) like birds
                about to take off. The film

cuts to magma, twister,
             flood. This is not,

they insist, about now:
　　　　　　they swagger through elms,

past boughs more bleached
　　　　　　than gold to sing & rhyme

not what's past or passing,
　　　　　　but *what's to come.*

Jump Around (House of Pain, 1992)
A Fan Speaks to an Overzealous Irishman:

Don'tcha just love how they have that loop

    of bagpipes in the background? It's all about

Irish pride! Ireland's in the house of hip hop!

    I have nothing against Ireland. I have no doubt

        that it's a pretty cool place. But what you're

hearing is the sound of a sax.

    No, man. These guys are all about their

heritage. I mean, really: sit back, relax,

    & watch the video. See Everlast's jersey?

        The *Celtics*. I love that they use bagpipes in rap.

I'm telling you, it's a sax.

    Wait... did you see

    that plaid flash of a kilt? & oh snap:

there go the bagpipes again! What a climax.

What a statement for Irish pride.

    It's a sax.

Nuthin But a G Thang (Dr. Dre, 1992)

The bass unpaints my wall as the looped synth unscrolls

    behind. But wait: what's wrong with my TV?

      So much of this video is blurry

           that I feel like I have cataracts. They blur

           someone robbing a girl of her

bikini. They blur Warren G's hands as he rolls

a joint. They even blur the logo

on Snoop's pristine baseball hat (as though

      somehow the sight of a seven leafed

           plant would burn holes in your eyes). People say

           the G is for *gangsta*, but the censors have made

      everything so out of focus (gotta keep

those dangerous sights from the masses)

it makes me think the G is for *glasses*.

Jump (Kris Kross, 1992)

The two twelve year old kids were playing

video games in an Atlanta Mall when they

> were asked for a moment of their time

> by a producer who'd hardly even heard them rhyme

before he offered them a deal. Thus were born

> the Mack Dad & Daddy Mack. Then it

came down to finding a song, & if House of Pain,

> Van Halen & The Pointer Sisters could make hits

about jumping, well then heck, so could they.

The two threw their clothes on backwards & made

> a video of themselves jumping all

> around like… kids. One day, they're just chillin' in the mall.

The next, they've got the whole town hopping.

Oh, the deals you can find when you go shopping.

Insane in the Brain (Cypress Hill, 1993)
Two scientists speak:

You've seen the video where B

Real touches the screen & it looks like it turns

to water, right?

        Are you asking me

if I was alive in the 90s? (Smirks)

Yeah, well I'm working on my own video

in the lab. You may have to squint,

but look: the dots change from beet red to yellow,

expanding & contracting with the different

frequencies of B Real's whine.

        Wasting

time again? Wait… you're telling me that's a *squid?*

        Hell

yeah. The close-up of its dorsal side. I'm testing

the effect of music on pigmented cells.

You said you were *working*, but the hell you were.

This membrane's insane! Man, this shit's cellular!

Gin and Juice (Snoop Doggy Dog, 1993)

The video goes back to when Snoop was Calvin
    Cordozar Broadus, empty-handed
in plaid pajamas. His parents ruin
    his morning when they tell him to get out of bed

& get a job, or at least take out the trash.
    When they step out the door, he slaps his cheeks
    & screams into the camera. Suddenly
we're left with *Home* (or Homeboy) *Alone*. Fast-

forward a few years: heavy-lidded, tall
    & thin as a hollowed out blunt, Snoop unreels
lyrics in his patented sleep-drugged drawl.
    He's got his own place now, & he'll

stay in if he wants to, in one hand some tonic
& Tanqueray, in one a fatty of chronic.

The Lost Tapes of *Crazy Wisdom Masters*
(Jungle Brothers, 1993)

N.Y. State of Mind (Nas, 1994)

In the studio, the beat floats
over the piano's loop: three bass notes

      descending, then a quick splay of treble.
      When someone pounds on the vocal

booth window, Nas turns his head & lip-
reads: *we're recording, man, let's get to it!*

      He lifts his lips to the mic & admits
      Man, *I don't know how to start this...*

Most would choose to have their indecision
cut. But later, because he knows that this is one

      part of what makes the music, Nas goes
      up to the producer in the booth: *hey, yo,*

it takes vision & improv to make a hit,
so keep this on the record. All of it.

Sabotage (Beastie Boys, 1994)

The sirened car guns
               through the suburbs

       against a dizzy
                   skyline, its tires

still spinning as the boys
                   leap out to the curb.

        Mike D rolls in the grass
                    as though on fire

then kicks down a gate
                as Ad-Rock wails (*I can't stand*

        it...) Authorized by fake
                    70s mustaches,

they scale buildings,
                leap over walls, land

        on the pavements grey
                    with their wigs & sunglasses

still perfectly aligned,
                all Starsky & Hutch.

        As the purple glow
                    of the mid-day sky

blazes between buildings,
                these MCs & cops must

know in their deep heart's core
               that they need to arise

& flow now, 'cause there'll always be,

               in this old town,

more beats & more bad guys

               to throw down.

Creep (TLC, 1995)

Left Eye gets released to work on the trio's

  second album (she's on probation

for the whole *throw my boyfriend's new shoes*

  in the tub, find some lighter fluid, drown

them & light them on fire trick) & the ladies

  record the song that would become the first single

for *CrazySexyCool*. Of the three,

  only Left Eye was against its release. A girl,

she said, should leave instead of cheating on her guy.

  In the video, she doesn't even mouth her

    background vocals. Weeks before, incensed

at the choice, the girl who wore condoms on her eye

  had threatened to wear black tape over

    her mouth, protection traded for abstinence.

Gangsta's Paradise (Coolio, 1995)

They say that Coolio was pissed when Weird
  Al Yankovic spoofed his lyrics
with "Amish Paradise," slipping on a black beard
  & hat for the shoot. But he himself had remixed

Stevie Wonder's song, updating it by
  twenty years by applying it to the gangsta
life. Stevie gave him everything: the high
  staccato strings, the signature

melody, & even the theme… They say
  the world has only five or six stories,
& we only repeat them, tweaking the way
  they're told. So, Coolio, this (& *every*) song is

just a reminder of the artist's age-old deal:
merely good musicians borrow. Great ones steal.

California Love (Tupac Shakur, 1995)

In the steel cage arena's main event

    Dre sports an eye patch & mohawk while Pac's

spike-studded getup (two shades more chic) compliments

       his trademark backwards handkerchief. The two are locked

into a fight to the death, but instead of gore

     & brute strength dictating the winner,

it's whoever can control the dance floor

       with their rhymes. They don't even need to wear

futuristic costumes to prove that the Thug Life

     can be dangerous; Tupac was shot

     the next year, his life untied because of a knot

of words. A gangsta's city is risky enough,

a vertical desert that each wanders alone,

this century's version of the Thunderdome.

Woo Hah!! (Busta Rhymes, 1996)

This is how it works: he signs the big deal,

    & then writer's block, like a swirling fog, blows

in for months. Day after day he feels

    numb, & he can't even bust a move, no

less a rhyme. So he decides to get

    his mind off it; he organizes a pickup

game, & he gets *into* it, his jaw set,

    his mouth wide as night as he drives to the hoop.

Then, mid-game, someone on the sidelines yells

    woo-hah!

        Busta runs off to find a pen,

& by the end of the weekend he's spilled

    enough ink for the entire album & then

some. It's about life's breaks, its fakes & pivots,

& how you can't write a lyric till you live it.

Going Back to Cali (Notorious BIG, 1997)

Cali sounds like the garden of Eden:
all palm trees & sun, & you've been forbidden

to go back due to some feud. Biggie
went back in his custom made Versace,

his coat big as a blanket. After the awards
show, he was rolling down the street towards

the next party, his Suburban's speakers playing
this very song: *whippin' on the freeway,*

the NYC way. Biggie knew
that there'd come a time when he'd have to

go back to the place where he'd die for a song.
& if you think Biggie's alone, you're wrong.

It'll happen to you, too, pal. We—
all of us—are going back to Cali.

Intergalactic (Beastie Boys, 1998)

The shot of the robot
                    plunging past a fleet

of pointillist stars quickly
                    cuts to the streets,

    a kimonoed woman
                        covering the O

    of her mouth. When the beat
                    starts, the heroes—

power plant suits
                with bright yellow nuclear

waste gloves & goggles—
                    fast forward

    through Tokyo as they dance
                        (it's more like stop-

    time, pseudo-karate)
                        & even the robot

can't help but gyrate.
                    There's no Sphinx but

    a giant squid-headed
                    monster slouching

toward the city. Its kick drains life
                    from the robot's

eyes. But when music revives him,
the robot slings

the squid into power lines.
The city's safe—Tokyo's center holds

for now—as the monster
sizzles in volts.

Everything is Everything (Lauryn Hill, 1999)

An enormous needle descends on New York
    like an alien invasion, & it seems
like the streets have been hit by an earthquake
    until you find that, beneath all the silent screams,

the city's been transformed into a giant
    record, which starts, now, to spin. As the needle
cruises the outskirts to the static chant
    of the pavement's car-laden groove, people stumble

to the ground, but L Boogie struts as though the streets
    lay absolutely still. The girl's got
more than balance. She's got flow. & in this city
    where even pigeons can get caught

in the round (man, even the zoo's *sloths* are busy)
it takes that & more to keep from getting dizzy.

2000s

Party Up (DMX, 2000)

It's a bad day to be DMX. All

the man wants to do is withdraw

    some cash, but the ATM's out of order.

        So he heads into the branch where he finds

    tellers & patrons alike sprawled out on the floor.

        When he's confused for the robber (he's dark skinned,

after all) & a SWAT team floods the street outside,

    he runs to the top of the building

    & phones his homie. By the time he flings

        himself over the side of the building a few

        Suburbans have pulled up, & ladies have piled out to

overwhelm the cops with their short skirts & grind.

Though DMX gets away, thanks to his call,

no one's ever suffered so much from a withdrawal.

Apollo Kids (Ghostface Killah, 2000)

When a supervisor on the phone vows

    that they're gonna have a high volume day

it sounds like he's talking about how

    loud the music will be. But no: he means that they

plan to pump out 50,000 kicks by

    the end of the shift. As Ghostface oversees

the factory where workers assemble his line

    of shoes, he & his words thunder through the aisles. But he

doesn't use a mic. Instead, he grips

    what looks to be a golden ice cream cone.

    Maybe it's because he'd just been diagnosed

as diabetic; so now he depends on hip-

hop's beats & the mic's constant hit of sugar.

The shoes are his business, but the mic's his cure.

Deception (Blackalicious, 2000)

Since writing limericks often prevents flow,

you have to like this rhyme experiment. No

doubt if they got stuck it's

'cause they weren't from Nantucket;

Blackalicious is from Sacramento.

Lose Yourself (Eminem, 2002)

In the freestyle battle scene in *8 Mile*
B Rabbit stands, scared & hollow-eyed, while

Doc stares him down. When the beat drops, he's frozen.
But then he launches into an F-bomb laden

rant in which he doesn't so much lose himself as
expound just why he's a loser: he's white trash,

he says, he lives in his mom's trailer,
he just got jumped, & his girl's been spreading her

legs around town. Doc stands there speechless. Nobody
can make fun of you if you've already

turned the dozens upon yourself. Rabbit had learned
that one way to win is by making sure you lose.

Turning flaws into art is like burning
an intricate tattoo around a stubborn bruise.

Work It (Missy Elliott, 2002)

It's not some unknown tribal language

or even Gibberish when Elliott

    hits you with her cataract of

poured syllables. It sounds like she's saying

    Itsyur fremma nemma swen yettu. But

if you play part of the chorus backward

    (it's as though the record were spitting the

riff right back) the sludge clarifies

    into language: *I put my thing down,*

    flip it & reverse it. She head-

spins like a baby blue screw then puckers her

lips & lifts her chin as if we couldn't

    hear her. We hear her: her voice is a

mirror of sound, refracting syllables like light.

My Block (Scarface, 2002)

This is what it's like to watch decades pass over

    a block in one seamless shot: someone

throwing shoes over a telephone wire

    while a woman gives birth to a son

on the sidewalk fast-forwards to kids break-

    dancing in track suits. Top rock fades

to lips locked in back of a car. Cops spray-

    paint someone in the eyes, & a ball game

bleeds into the wind-tossed candles

    of a funeral. The billboard reads: *What is in*

the beginning will be in the end. But all

    the people are gone. The only thing

that remains the same after the crossfire

of the years is the shoes hanging from the wire.

In Da Club (50 Cent, 2003)

In the secret desert compound, Dre
    & Eminem stand in long white
lab coats, clutching clipboards. This is how they
    look when they're discovering a new hit,

a new sensation, a new element on
    hip hop's periodic table: two rogue
scientists watching, on the far side of the one-
    way glass, the creation of a cyborg

who they'll admit into their club. They shut
    the tiny door in Fiddy's back, & he's
ready to demonstrate his strength not
    only on the treadmill but with his

lyrics. *My flow brought me the dough*
he boasts, but it looks like someone else's show.

Hey Ya (Outkast, 2003)

Eight versions of Andre 3000 cascade

    across the stage: he plays bass, drums, guitar, keyboards

& sings with the trio who look like they'd

    been snatched away from an afternoon of horse-

back riding. Some say that the video's based

    on The Beatles' 1964

Ed Sullivan Show. True enough, girls just off stage

    scream. Some faint & are carried out the door.

The band's outfits are muted to grey

    on the black & white screens, dulling the sequins'

blur. They're *just* like The Beatles. Except there are eight

    of them. Oh, & they're black. Well, & since they're Georgians,

it's not really the British who are invading.

Still, aren't the parallels fascinating?

Ch-Check It Out (Beastie Boys, 2004)

In the wake of the smoke,
                the two towers down,

      they rap of a fused
                      city unfurling

from the ashes, a far
                cry from the clowning

     of girls, all I really
                   want is girls…

Now, even their jokes
                speak volumes. *Check*

     it out: in the clip,
                    they materialize

on the street in shiny
                tight Star Trek

     gear. But when their work
                    is done they realize

that no magic word—
                no *shazam* or

     abracadabra—can beam them
                  up to their ship.

With their ladders gone,
                most would feel in a jam or

screwed. But the boys are content

        in the rag & bone shop

of the streets: the towers

        down, the shaken

crowds dispersing, the city

        ambushed but unbroken.

99 Problems (Jay-Z, 2004)

The room, full of chanting volunteers

    at the end of an election cycle,

shimmies & bounces to bass & better years

    ahead: Jay-Z is playing to the full

house of Obama's staff, changing the lyrics

    to *99 problems but a Bush ain't one.*

    At last, they say, the country's done

with those eight years (the sequel to Reaganomics).

Now they can party to the rhythmic

    pulse of bass designed to break the Richter scale,

    the rhymes just loud enough to drown the wail

of the past month's attack ads. If you don't like

what they say, then you can add your word.

 If you don't like the past *you can press fast forward.*

Get Back (Ludacris, 2004)

When a fool named Money recognizes
    Ludacris at the urinals, he insists
    that he'd make a great manager. Ludacris'
forearms & hands are so oversized

that his wrists look as thick as his waist.
    It wouldn't take much for him to do
some damage. So when Money gets in his face
    Luda lets the would-be manager know just who

he's dealing with. *Get back*, he screams,
    then he busts his massive fist through a brick wall.
Ludacris would do *nothing* for Money,
    which is why, I guess, he started this brawl.

This Popeye's not looking for a dime
or even spinach. He gets his strength from rhymes.

How We Do (The Game, 2004)

A Compton Blood, The Game opened his door

    to make a routine sale & was greeted

with five bullets. When he awoke almost four

    days later, he was hounded by a sudden need

to hear & study dozens of vintage

    hip hop albums. Once he recovered, he made

a mix tape—*You Know What It Is*—which

    circulated around town till it found Dre.

Soon the Game swapped his pad for a multi-million

dollar crib. Since then he's said *fuck this mansion.*

    Fuck these cars. You're not gonna fit

    none of this shit in a casket.

Still, his song insists that you don't have it made

'til you've got Lamborghini doors on your Escalade.

Touch the Sky (Kanye West, 2005)

For days we'd seen footage of the hurricane

    pummeling the Louisiana coast:

flooding, the poor dispossessed, more rain,

    & people waving from roofs. The state was a ghost

of itself. Cut to: the Katrina fund drive

    where Mike Meyers & Kanye plead for donations.

At first they stick to the script. Then, on live

    camera, West—who can blame him?—comes undone

& stutters into an ad lib: *Bush doesn't care*

    about black people. The spot unravels

to the chasm between millionaires

    & the homeless.

                Months later, on MTV, Evel

Kanyevel eyes a canyon, steeling himself

before trying to jump an unbridgeable gulf.

Mr. Carter (L'il Wayne, 2008)

The album cover features a pensive

    baby with L'il Wayne's signature tattoos:

        his wide-open eyes conceal the *Fear*

& God on his eyelids, though the cursive

        of stands out like an intricate bindi, & tears

like purple jewels adorn his cheeks.

    Throughout his life Mr. Carter's bound to lose

friends, family, lovers, & eventually

        his own breath, but these tats he'll *never* be without.

        If you could hold onto two things & never

    let them go, what would they be? One palm shouts

        gun in wine-dark ink, & the other

whispers *the world*, so that he can

always say he has them in his hands.

Rising Down (The Roots, 2008)

It's not what you'd expect to hear when you go
      to the mall, but there it is: the repeated
chime to shake us out of our slumber: *hello*
      hello hello hello. The rhythm creeps

along, the opposite of the shoppers rushing
      from store to store, balancing ziggurats
      of boxes in this season of want. Yeah, so what,
it's 80 degrees in Alaska? Just airbrush

      the ice back in. You still need to get your
      Super Laser Blaster Retaliator.
So go ahead & pay, then hold out
your hands to receive the future you've bought.

      & no offense, sir, I don't mean to be drastic,
      but *how you want it bagged, paper or plastic?*

What I Am (Will.i.am, 2010)

So Will.i.am blackens his face

    for his appearance with Nicki Minaj's

crew when they sing *Check It Out* at the VMAs,

    & the next morning everyone's talking because

it looked too much like blackface.

                News flash: Will's

    got a black face with black paint or not.

    Weeks later, when he unveils a new cut

on Sesame Street (season 41!), he'll

be surrounded by a swaying rainbow

    of puppets: Grover lifting his string-thin

arms, Big Bird tilting back & forth, thrown

    like a storm-tossed tree. & there'll be no headlines

the next day that Cookie Monster's head

looked more blue or Elmo's looked more red.

Make Some Noise (Beastie Boys, 2011)

The three, hopping out
                of a girl-filled limo &

    swiping champagne
                  from a restaurant, stall

before the DeLorean.
                 The "wind" is a canned

    Western effect, the wolf
                  & raven calls

alien in the cityscape.
                Then out steps—*poof!*—

    their future selves. Awkward
                  silence, then the two

groups—six B-Boys—
                 have words. For the dance-off

    they lay down the mat
                  & get down to

work: simple top rocking
                leads to the windmill,

    the worm… Rap, you might think,
                  is no country

for old men, but this dance floor
                shows they got it still,

though *grandpa*
        been rappin' since '83.

Old men are just coats on a stick
        unless they prove

that the kids they were
        can show them new moves.

NOTES

1980s & before:

The Apache Loop (DJ Kool Herc, 1975): The version of Apache that the Incredible Bongo Band made in 1973 became the classic break thanks to DJs like Kool Herc and Afrika Bambaataa. Kool Herc's greatest claim to fame is that he was the first to isolate and loop breaks by spinning two copies of the same record on separate turntables.

Rapper's Delight (Sugarhill Gang, 1979): The story goes that Hank Jackson auditioned for Sylvia Robinson in a car outside the pizzeria where he worked, and she immediately offered him a job. Apparently, before he worked with Michael (Wonder Mike) Wright and Guy (Master Gee) O'Brien in the studio, he pocketed the lyrics of his friend, Grandmaster Caz, many of which show up in the song. The lyrics overlay Chic's hit "Good Times."
Hank didn't actually go right from the audition to the studio, as it happens in the poem. While we're at it, Sugar Hill Records wasn't really "big time" yet either.

Can I Get a Soul Clap (Grand Wizard Theodore, 1980) Grand Wizard Theodore is credited as the first DJ to scratch. As described in the poem, the discovery was an accident. The italicized thought at the end of the poem is, of course, pure conjecture.

Flash to the Beat (Grandmaster Flash, 1982): Grandmaster Flash created the first crossfade, which allowed a DJ to move more seamlessly between two records. And yes, when I say "Frankenstein," I really mean "Frankenstein's monster."

Looking For the Perfect Beat (Afrika Bambaataa,1983): Afrika Bambaataa was the first to call this burgeoning music "hip hop." He famously transformed his street gang, the Black Spades, into the b-boys of the Zulu Nation.
Details about Bambaataa's French tour were taken from *Can't Stop Won't Stop, A History of the Hip-Hop Generation*, by Jeff Chang.

Fight for your Right (Beastie Boys, 1986): This song, like all seven Beastie Boy poems in this collection (one from each of the albums on which they rap), is linked to a poem by W.B. Yeats. In "Among School Children," Yeats asks, "how can we know the dancer from the dance?" I've always been interested in how intelligent people can project such stupid personas. The Beastie Boys, despite the misogynistic and alcoholic characters they portrayed early in their recording careers, have grown to be some of the more compassionate and aware musicians out there. But, as in Yeats' analogy of the dancer, how the heck are we supposed to distinguish the idiots from the sympathetic humans when they both inhabit the same frames? I consider the seven of these poems a series, entitled, "What Rough Beasties."

Rhyme Pays (Ice T, 1987): This is the first song to have a parental advisory sticker.

Pump Up the Jam (Technotronic, 1989): Of course there's no evidence that the frantically shifting images of video were created specifically to cover up Kellingi's lack of English, but it makes a nice theory.

Potholes in My Lawn (De La Soul, 1989): Yes, De La Soul is from Amityville, but to be honest I'm not sure that the media ever hounded them about it. In this fictional interview, the reporter is unable to get over the fact.

High Plains Drifter (Beastie Boys, 1989): This poem references the fire that burned down the famous Paul's Boutique, a photo of which is featured on the cover of the Beastie Boys' second album. The poem also alludes to Yeats' "Leda and the Swan," which retells the popular Greek myth of how Zeus took the form of a swan and assaulted a woman named Leda while in flight, then let her drop. Yeats asks whether Leda had enough time to "put on (Zeus') knowledge with his power/ before the indifferent beak could let her drop." Because of the fire theme, I was thinking of the Hindu myth of Agni and Soma. Agni represents all that burns, and Soma represents all that is burned. Everything in the world is one or the other, if not both. When I eat a bowl of soup, I'm Agni, and the soup is the Soma. But at the same time, I'm Soma, because Time is Agni, eating me. And so on…

1990s:

U Can't Touch This (MC Hammer, 1990): MC Hammer really does have a waterfall in his mansion. Because why not?

So What'cha Want (Beastie Boys, 1992): This poem was filtered through Yeats' "Sailing to Byzantium."

Jump (Kris Kross, 1992): I've read a number of versions of how Jermaine Dupri discovered Kris Kross. Every version includes the mall. I'm partial to the image of Dupri walking up to them while they're playing video games.

Insane in the Brain (Cypress Hill, 1993): The scientists are from a group called Backyard Brains, which focuses on neurobiology. Seriously. Search this video out.

The Lost Tapes of Crazy Wisdom Masters (Jungle Brothers, 1993): Most of the songs on Crazy Wisdom Masters were lost. Mike G is quoted as saying that the reels just disappeared sometime during the process of mixing that album.

N.Y. State of Mind (Nas, 1994): The final lines of the poem, spoken by Nas, are pure conjecture. In fact, "Keep this on the record, all of it," is a quote from another recording all together. In the famous session of Miles Davis and The Jazz Giants, Davis yells these words up to Rudy Van Gelder, who is recording the session. My buddy Sascha Feinstein has written a better poem than this, "Christmas Eve," which also ends with these lines. So I owe a debt to him.

Sabotage (Beastie Boys, 1994): This Beastie Boys poem is filtered through Yeats' "The Lake Isle of Innisfree."

Gangsta's Paradise (Coolio, 1995): T.S. Eliot was famously supposed to have said that good poets borrow and great ones steal.

Going back to Cali (Notorious BIG, 1997): According to some sources, this was the song playing in Biggie's car when he was shot.

Intergalactic (Beastie Boys, 1998): This poem is filtered through Yeats' "The Second Coming."

2000s:

Apollo Kids (Ghostface Killah, 2000): Ghostface discovered that he was diabetic in 1996.

Deception (Blackalicious, 2000): "Deception" is written in a string of what could loosely be defined as limericks. Although the first, second and fifth lines rhyme, traditionally, the shorter third and fourth lines rhyme, too.

Work It (Missy Elliott, 2002): In honor of the backwards lines in this song, I've used a "backwards" rhyme scheme, in which the rhymes appear at the start of the lines instead of the end.

Ch-Check It Out (Beastie Boys, 2004): This poem is filtered through Yeats' "The Circus Animals' Desertion."

How We Do (The Game, 2004): Here's The Game's full quote: "Fuck this mansion. Fuck these cars. I would jump back in a Cutlass tomorrow, man. I don't care about this materialistic shit. You can't fit none of this in a casket." And actually, 50 Cent raps the lines about Lamborghini doors on escalade.

Make Some Noise (Beastie Boys, 2011): This poem is filtered through Yeats' "Sailing to Byzantium."

CPSIA information can be obtained at www.ICGtesting.com
Printed in the USA
LVOW04s2009290115

424894LV00015B/947/P